BORN TO BE KING
Prince William of Wales

BORN TO BE KING
Prince William of Wales

The Prince of Wales' Coat of Arms, which Prince William will inherit when he succeeds to the title. The Royal Arms have been adapted and the Welsh Dragon and Prince of Wales' Feathers have been added, along with the motto, which means "I Serve".

text by Trevor Hall

Designed by Philip Clucas MSIAD

Produced by Ted Smart and David Gibbon

Colour Library Books

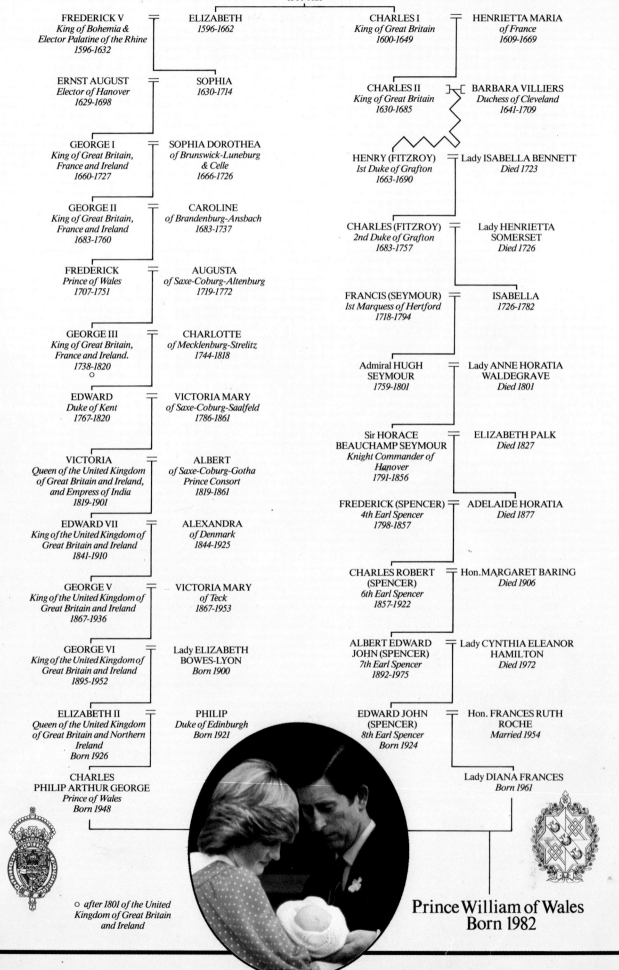

JAMES VI and I
King of England, Scotland, France and Ireland
1566-1625

FREDERICK V
King of Bohemia & Elector Palatine of the Rhine
1596-1632
=
ELIZABETH
1596-1662

CHARLES I
King of Great Britain
1600-1649
=
HENRIETTA MARIA
of France
1609-1669

ERNST AUGUST
Elector of Hanover
1629-1698
=
SOPHIA
1630-1714

CHARLES II
King of Great Britain
1630-1685
=
BARBARA VILLIERS
Duchess of Cleveland
1641-1709

GEORGE I
King of Great Britain, France and Ireland
1660-1727
=
SOPHIA DOROTHEA
of Brunswick-Luneburg & Celle
1666-1726

HENRY (FITZROY)
1st Duke of Grafton
1663-1690
—
Lady ISABELLA BENNETT
Died 1723

GEORGE II
King of Great Britain, France and Ireland
1683-1760
=
CAROLINE
of Brandenburg-Ansbach
1683-1737

CHARLES (FITZROY)
2nd Duke of Grafton
1683-1757
=
Lady HENRIETTA SOMERSET
Died 1726

FREDERICK
Prince of Wales
1707-1751
=
AUGUSTA
of Saxe-Coburg-Altenburg
1719-1772

FRANCIS (SEYMOUR)
1st Marquess of Hertford
1718-1794
=
ISABELLA
1726-1782

GEORGE III
King of Great Britain, France and Ireland.
1738-1820
○
=
CHARLOTTE
of Mecklenburg-Strelitz
1744-1818

Admiral HUGH SEYMOUR
1759-1801
=
Lady ANNE HORATIA WALDEGRAVE
Died 1801

EDWARD
Duke of Kent
1767-1820
=
VICTORIA MARY
of Saxe-Coburg-Saalfeld
1786-1861

Sir HORACE BEAUCHAMP SEYMOUR
Knight Commander of Hanover
1791-1856
=
ELIZABETH PALK
Died 1827

VICTORIA
Queen of the United Kingdom of Great Britain and Ireland, and Empress of India
1819-1901
=
ALBERT
of Saxe-Coburg-Gotha Prince Consort
1819-1861

FREDERICK (SPENCER)
4th Earl Spencer
1798-1857
=
ADELAIDE HORATIA
Died 1877

EDWARD VII
King of the United Kingdom of Great Britain and Ireland
1841-1910
=
ALEXANDRA
of Denmark
1844-1925

CHARLES ROBERT (SPENCER)
6th Earl Spencer
1857-1922
=
Hon. MARGARET BARING
Died 1906

GEORGE V
King of the United Kingdom of Great Britain and Ireland
1867-1936
=
VICTORIA MARY
of Teck
1867-1953

ALBERT EDWARD JOHN (SPENCER)
7th Earl Spencer
1892-1975
=
Lady CYNTHIA ELEANOR HAMILTON
Died 1972

GEORGE VI
King of the United Kingdom of Great Britain and Ireland
1895-1952
=
Lady ELIZABETH BOWES-LYON
Born 1900

ELIZABETH II
Queen of the United Kingdom of Great Britain and Northern Ireland
Born 1926
=
PHILIP
Duke of Edinburgh
Born 1921

EDWARD JOHN (SPENCER)
8th Earl Spencer
Born 1924
=
Hon. FRANCES RUTH ROCHE
Married 1954

CHARLES PHILIP ARTHUR GEORGE
Prince of Wales
Born 1948

Lady DIANA FRANCES
Born 1961

○ *after 1801 of the United Kingdom of Great Britain and Ireland*

Prince William of Wales
Born 1982

The appearance of Halley's Comet in 1066 was immediately followed by the death of King Harold, and the Norman conquest of England. William of Normandy was said to have remarked to his courtiers that "a comet like this was only seen when a kingdom wanted a king!" Just how would William have interpreted the arrival of his namesake, Prince William, just eight hours after a solar eclipse (11.52 a.m. G.M.T. June 21st)? It certainly suggests an out-of-the-ordinary personality and fate, a Prince whose name will go down in history.

Being a Cancer subject, Prince William has an emotionally based personality, affectionate, sympathetic, protective. He is deeply committed psychologically to his mother in particular, to his family in general. He is "clan conscious". Conservative in thought and basically cautious in action, though not without enterprise, he is predisposed towards the development of strong ties and convictions, and strong prejudices too. These qualities will be combined with an uncanny intuition which will enable him to read minds, anticipate actions.

Sagittarius on the Ascendant of his chart suggests an element of restlessness, a liking for travel, variety and change, and also a basic cheerfulness, sociability and optimism. Yet, because Neptune is also on the Ascendant and in opposition to both Sun and Moon, he is shy and sensitive, has quick sympathies, is prone to over-emotionalism, and can be quickly moved to both laughter and tears. This draws attention to a complexity in his personality. Mars being in close aspect to his Sun and Moon, he has a goodly share of courage, ambition, aggression and physical vitality, quite a temper and a vein of foolhardiness. In childhood, this combination will make him moody and prone to tantrums because he feels deeply and responds aggressively. In maturity, it will make him a man to be reckoned with; one who combines subtlety with a capacity for decisive and forceful action.

Because he is second in line to the throne of England, the positioning of Jupiter on the midheaven of the horoscope is of vital significance. Throughout the reigns of the Houses of Saxe-Coburg-Gotha, Hanover, Brunswick or Windsor, every monarch without exception has had Saturn and Jupiter prominent in their horoscopes. Prince William's horoscope has the hallmark of monarchy, whereas his father Prince Charles' lacks this distinctive feature, as did King Edward VIII, the Duke of Windsor's.

A good I.Q. and a useful academic ability is indicated, but it is an intellect which is imaginative and artistic, which inclines towards idealism and perfectionism, rather than being pragmatic, analytical or rational. He is specifically not a mathematician, technician or scientist. His talent is for the arts. He is capable of being highly imaginative and will veer towards the world of fantasy, tending to think on a larger than life scale. His ready sympathies and his emotionalism will make him a romantic, gullible, susceptible to flattery, a "good fellow"

Prince William has an affinity for the sea. He will continue the family association with the Royal Navy which has existed for several generations. Yet, more than most members of the royal family, he has intellectual capabilities. He leans towards being an academic. There will be sound sense in giving him a legal grounding; he could develop an interest in constitutional law.

No fewer than four planets are positioned in the Ninth House of his horoscope, that section which has to do with religion, the law and overseas matters. This suggests the possibility of strong religious convictions but not necessarily harmonious relationships with the established church, that his reign will be notable for turbulent foreign relationships, and that there is an element of risk to his health and well-being when travelling and living overseas.

Not only because he is a prince, but because he has great charm, is sensitive, sympathetic and responsive as well as full of vitality, he will wreak havoc with feminine hearts and this could become much publicised because the strong Neptune element in his horoscope predisposes him to involvement in scandal. Anticipate a first serious love affair when he is in his early 20's (around 2003 AD) but do not be surprised if, as in his father's case, marriage is delayed until he is in his 30's. Without doubt he will be conformist in his choice of marriage partner, but there is an astrological question mark over the health of this partner after marriage and there is a possibility that he will marry more than once.

The astrological picture is therefore of an affectionate, sensitive yet lively child, courageous and possessing a vein of aggression which will flare from time to time. He will need, and demand, a lot of affection and attention, being prone to vivid emotional experiences. There will be a complete and willing integration into his family and a psychological dependence on family affection and approval. He is fortunate to be born into a closely knit family. The liking that recent generations of royals have shown for country life will be present in his make-up and in time he will develop a keen interest in the royal stables, in horse racing and breeding.

A good I.Q. will enable him to do well scholastically, and he will show a liking for water sports. He is well orientated, psychologically, to being a royal and to the discipline, responsibility and involvement in ceremony that this involves. In maturity he will have a vigorous, active disposition and will be capable of becoming a considerable statesman, combining keen intuition and a feel for public mood and reaction with a useful capacity for leadership. Insofar as royals are permitted to, Prince William will show an active interest in the table—in food and drink—and be something of a gourmet. He could, in time, become a little too fond of the bottle!

He is highly unlikely to remain an only child—a sister will appear on the scene in 1984. It is rumoured that the Prince and Princess of Wales fancy a larger home. Prince Charles' horoscope strongly suggests the possibility of a move to a new home in a new location in late 1984 or early 1985. Yet the most interesting indication in regard to Prince William's future occurs in the late 1980's. Both he and his mother, the Princess of Wales, are Cancer subjects. Between 1985

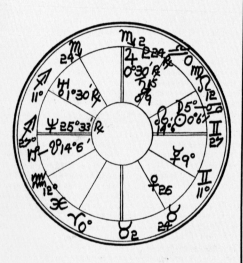

Hour: 9.03 p.m.
Date: 21st June 1982
Place: London.

NHS Number	LSBSS 115	**BIRTH**	Entry No. **115**

		Administrative area
Registration district	Westminster	
Sub-district	Westminster	City of Westminster

CHILD

1. Date and place of birth	Twenty first June 1982 St. Marys Hospital Praed Street Westminster

		3. Sex
2. Name and surname	His Royal Highness Prince William Arthur Philip Louis	Male

FATHER

4. Name and surname	His Royal Highness Prince Charles Philip Arthur George Prince of Wales
5. Place of birth	Westminster
6. Occupation	Prince of the United Kingdom

MOTHER

7. Name and surname	Her Royal Highness The Princess of Wales
8. Place of birth	Sandringham Norfolk

9.(a) Maiden surname	SPENCER	(b) Surname at marriage if different from maiden surname —

10. Usual address (if different from place of child's birth)	Highgrove Near Tetbury Gloucestershire

INFORMANT

11. Name and surname (if not the mother or father) —	12. Qualification Father

13. Usual address (if different from that in 10 above) —

14. I certify that the particulars entered above are true to the best of my knowledge and belief

Charles

.... Signature of informant

15. Date of registration Nineteenth July 1982	16. Signature of registrar Joan V. Webb Registrar

17. Name given after registration, and surname

In the chill, eerie, half-lit dawn of the first day of an English summer, a royal-blue Rover police car glided effortlessly through the gates of Kensington Palace and sped towards the unfashionable, littered streets of Paddington. Its occupants – like most of their fellow-countrymen, rarely astir at such an hour – were a chauffeur, a personal detective and, sitting in the back as comfortably as circumstances would allow, the heir to the Throne of the United Kingdom and his 20-year-old wife.

An hour beforehand, she had entered into the early stages of labour, and the minutely-planned arrangements for her confinement were being put in hand with all the care and precision of a military parade. A drive of only ten minutes separated the Palace from the royal destination but, as always in the mental panic of an incipient first labour, it seemed there was not a moment to lose. The immediate objectives had been to alert the Queen's gynaecologist, Mr George Pinker, and to ensure that a room and the necessary nursing staff were on hand to receive the mother-to-be into hospital care for the duration. As if at the touch of Lord Maclean's guiding hand, fresh from the triumph of last year's meticulously-organised Royal Wedding, these much more personal and totally private strategies succeeded, and shortly after five o'clock Diana, Princess of Wales was admitted to the Lindo Wing of St Mary's hospital, Paddington. And for once in her twenty-one months in the glare of publicity, there was not a photographer to be seen.

There can be few less romantic districts within a stone's throw of Central London than the Praed Street area of Paddington, and the grimy, rambling hospital which dominates the west end of the street proclaims and reinforces the sullen atmosphere with immovable Victorian dejection. The most celebrated of its extensions, the Lindo Wing, is hardly more prepossessing, with its cold, forbidding exterior typifying the failed classicism of nineteen-thirties architecture. In the days of its construction, however, it seemed the ultimate not only in design but also in the scope and quality of the facilities it offered, and on its completion in 1938 the hospital Trustees had asked Queen

Elizabeth to open it. Little could she have guessed as she did so that forty-four years later her own grandson would bring his wife here and that the eyes of the whole nation would focus on those double doors at the South Wharf Street entrance, hoping and praying for the safe delivery of a second heir in direct line of succession to the Throne.

As soon as Buckingham Palace released the news of the Princess' arrival a steady stream of onlookers – loyal, sentimental or merely curious – began to fill the barrier-lined pavements almost as

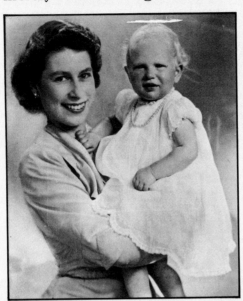

promptly as conscripts. The nation's Press – and through their agency the Press of the whole world – got early wind of the prospects and for a time it was difficult to judge whether they or the ordinary citizens and tourists of London had the monopoly of pavement area. By ten o'clock the first flowers had arrived – a tray of bright yellow freesias offering a welcome burst of colour to a grey

Prince Charles with his mother at Clarence House, and with his nanny Mabel Anderson in 1951. The pram was bought in 1926, when his mother was born.

morning and giving photographers their first real chance to exercise their cameras. The floral tributes reflected the wide range of wellwishers: there was everything from the massive baskets bristling with blooms from large commercial firms and institutions, to the single roses from individuals such as Tina Rawlins from Queensway, just two miles distant, and Dr Wayne Swift, New York psychotherapist, dealer in royal ephemera, a lifelong admirer of Prince Charles, and cock-a-hoop at the happy coincidence of being in London on this of all days.

By midday hardly anyone awake in the entire country was left in ignorance of the morning's news and London's lunch-hour saw the crowds swelled to bursting point with office and shop workers, torn between the demands of curiosity and peckishness, opting for the former. Press crews ran a constant relay to supply themselves with coffee and sandwiches, while an enterprising team of girls plied up

Princess Elizabeth, photographed by Marcus Adams in 1928 (above); with her mother, then Duchess of York, the same year (right), and with her grandmother Queen Mary in 1927. She was christened Elizabeth Alexandra Mary.

and down the crammed pavements offering strawberries and cream at monstrous prices. Well, it was after all the first day of Wimbledon. The Queen, who had left London with some reluctance that morning to visit the Royal Air Force in Cambridgeshire, with Prince Philip, ordered a special radio link to be set up on board her Andover aircraft so that she could be informed at the first sign of hard news. Her beaming smiles throughout the visit announced her unremitting joy at the prospect of being a grandmother for the third time, while also concealing her understandable preoccupation with the significance of the day in the history of her dynasty.

But at St Mary's there were only comings and goings. A succession of false alarms never failed to keep everyone on their toes, and the longer it all went on the more determined everyone was to stay there till the bitter end. Bitter it was too, as cold showers of rain belied the time of year, but while Prince Charles remained within, the supposed imminence of the royal birth lost none of its credibility. News cameras ranged up and along the uniform lines of

the hospital's windows, vainly searching for tell-tale activity. All they recorded were off-duty staff peering back at the crowd below, which in turn peered hopefully at the doorway of the Lindo Wing. All were locked in the inescapable fascination of waiting. Radio bulletins confirmed the standstill every hour on the hour, their reporters standing frozen on the windswept roadway to relate the news vacuum for the sake of journalistic immediacy. Early evening television news programmes led with a hint of impatience – "Still no

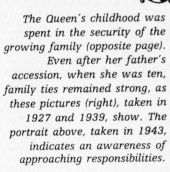

The Queen's childhood was spent in the security of the growing family (opposite page). Even after her father's accession, when she was ten, family ties remained strong, as these pictures (right), taken in 1927 and 1939, show. The portrait above, taken in 1943, indicates an awareness of approaching responsibilities.

news from St Mary's Hospital . . ." – and doggedly embellished the non-event with reports of the day's proceedings, interviews with onlookers and assurances that lengthy labours were the norm for first-born children.

As the BBC television newsreaders prepared to repeat the

Princess Elizabeth was 22 when these official pictures were taken in 1948 and early 1949. The Princess of Wales' baby was born shortly before her twenty-first birthday, for which Lord Snowdon took this excellent picture (opposite).

procedure for the Nine O'Clock News that evening they had no reason to suspect that the Princess was in fact on the verge of a delivery. The news that there was no news was thus no sooner imparted than it became instantly out of date. At precisely 9.03 pm on Monday 21st June 1982, and after sixteen hours' labour, Britain's ninth Princess of Wales gave birth to a son. He weighed 7lbs 1½oz, had blue eyes, fair to blondish hair, cried lustily (as all babies do) and was, as Prince Charles joyously announced, "in marvellous form."

From within the hospital, telephone calls were hastily made to Buckingham Palace and to Grosvenor Square, where Earl Spencer has his London pied-à-terre. The Queen, safely back from the East Midlands, was said to be "absolutely delighted" at the news. Lord

17

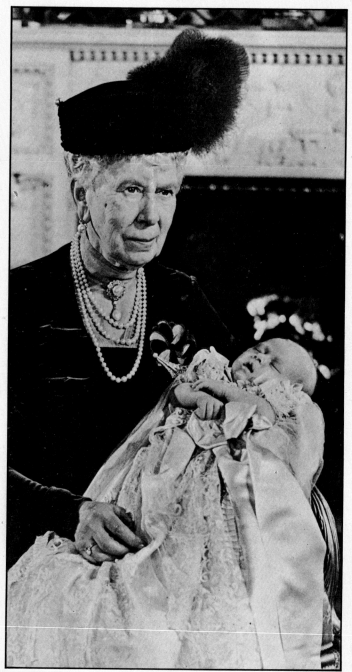

Spencer, now grandfather to a future King of Great Britain and Northern Ireland, went one better and actually appeared on the steps of his home, fairly bubbling with suppressed excitement, saying how happy he was to be part of this historic occasion and how lucky the baby was to have Diana for a mother. The Duke of Edinburgh, busy with half a week's engagements in Cambridge, was still hoping, three days after the birth, for an opportunity "to see him eventually." The Queen Mother, who in anticipation of the event had travelled up from Royal Lodge Windsor to Clarence House that evening, said she was overjoyed, while at the Palace Theatre in the West End, where

Princess Margaret attended the musical "Song and Dance" the audience rose to its feet and applauded rapturously when the star of the show, Wayne Sleep, announced the news after the finale. Other members of the Royal Family were contacted less easily: Prince Edward was still at Gordonstoun, Prince Andrew was on board *HMS Invincible* after the successful recapture of the Falkland Islands, and Princess Anne, whose reaction to the news was the most

At his christening on 15th December 1948, Prince Charles is held by his great-grandmother Queen Mary (far left), his grandmother Queen Elizabeth (left) and his mother (above). (Right) with his own son in Lord Snowdon's happy family portrait.

memorable for being the least enthusiastic, was on an official tour of Texas and Colorado.

Tributes from a wider circle began to pour in. Dr Robert Runcie, the Archbishop of Canterbury, welcomed the tidings as fervently as he had celebrated the marriage of the royal couple eleven months previously: "We rejoice with them," he said. Cardiff, of which both the Prince and Princess are freemen, was said by its Lord Mayor to "hold them both very dear to our hearts," while further congratulations came in from the Roman Catholic Archbishop of Liverpool and from the Prime Minister. In the Commons, spontaneous cheering prompted the Speaker to voice the House's evident pleasure and to promise another time for its formal expression. While he turned the House's attention to the next item – that of Northern Ireland – a group of Conservatives were already putting together a motion which wished the Prince and Princess "every possible happiness in the future." The Lutine Bell would be rung at Lloyd's next day – one of the rare occasions when it heralds joyful tidings – and Fleet Street set out with its traditional verve to celebrate in print. Both the leader writer of the *Daily Telegraph* and William Hickey of the *Daily Express* hit on the idea of penning their own versions of a typical Betjeman nativity ode: the absence of the customary lyric tribute from the Poet Laureate, unwell at 76 years of age, gave them ample scope to rhapsodise about the great event

"Hard by the Western Region Terminus
At Paddington – high point of railway art.
..."

Other newspaper writers passed a similarly active night. At one extreme the Court Circular was being adapted to take in the cold,

Four generations at Prince Charles' christening (above right) include Queen Mary and King George VI. (Above far right) with his parents in 1949; in this pram (top), and with his mother and sister Anne (above) in 1951. (Opposite) the fifth generation: Diana with her firstborn.

formal announcement, which *The Times* ran unceremoniously sandwiched between Prince Philip's visit to Churchill College and the Duke of Gloucester's trip to Portsmouth to inspect *HMS Nelson*. At the other extreme the horoscope compilers, impotent while the new Prince's star sign hovered between Gemini and Cancer, depending on which part of the day he would be born in, now scribbled themselves into an astrological frenzy with talk of new moons and planetary cusps.

Buckingham Palace made the official announcement within an hour of the birth. It came in the time-honoured way which thousands of people had anticipated by crowding outside the Palace railings all evening. A notice, framed in solid, highly-polished wood, was brought out and secured to the gates shortly before ten o'clock. In an age of instant everything it was almost predictable that it should have been pre-typed and pre-signed by the four doctors, only the precise timing of the birth being hastily written in by hand. It said, simply and in the impersonal manner of nearly all royal proclamations: "Her Royal Highness the Princess of Wales was safely delivered of a son at 9.03 pm today. Her Royal Highness and her child are both doing well." The crowds jostled to see the news, but it spread more quickly and effectively by word of mouth. Up went the flags and the cheers, and out rang the songs from loyal supporters of the Throne elated by the rich and satisfactory reward of their hours-long wait. Outside St Mary's Hospital a chorus of

singing, whistling and clapping greeted the announcement. Champagne bottles appeared from nowhere, were cracked open, and a lot of people got wet as a result. News reporters and cameramen cruised along the solid line of people, inviting comments and reactions to the news, but most of the answers were inaudible against the overwhelming swell of choruses of "For He's A Jolly Good Fellow" and chants – variations on a footballing theme – of "Nice One Charlie – Give Us Another One." To complete the picture a

Contrast in styles. The Queen's young family in 1950 (right); a formal pose against a domestic background. (Opposite) an informal Prince Charles with Diana and Prince William, their son and heir. (Above) Princess Anne with her mother in September 1950.

thumbsucking, rattle-waving doctor and nurse streaked down the road wearing adult-sized nappies.

Endless groups of additional sightseers now swelled the crowds as the possibility increased of a personal appearance by the proud father, and the persistent and deafening tumult made it clear to those inside the hospital – and to Prince Charles himself – that nothing less would persuade them to be on their way. Eventually the inevitable happened – though it was in fact more than that. Not only was the Prince seen in public for the first time that day – he proceeded to dive into the crowds to receive congratulations, hand-shakes and kisses from admirers high on the national celebration. Some people noticed that he had come out with a lipstick mark on

22

his cheek: before long there were one or two more. When he at length spoke, it was in superlatives, as only an occasion like this might justify. The baby, he said, was "beautiful" and "in marvellous form" and he himself was "relieved and delighted" and duly impressed by the experience of attending the birth. When he was asked about the likelihood of another baby a surprised, involuntary

"Bloody hell" escaped his lips. "Give us a chance," he added. "You ask my wife. I don't think she'll be too pleased just yet." He apologised for having kept everybody waiting for so long, intimated that although he and the Princess had thought of a couple of names, there was still some argument about it, and thanked everyone with warmth and sincerity for their interest and concern.

Then, with some difficulty which he was prepared on this occasion to tolerate, he disappeared into his blue Ford Granada estate car, and was whisked off to Kensington Palace. The entire complement of gazing humanity, fulfilled if not satiated with the fruits of its crusade and vigil, vanished almost as quickly into the night, and St Mary's was left to its habitual unwatched existence. It was 11.30 pm, and very nearly the end of the longest day of the year.

It was also the end of the most publicly monitored and the most exhaustively discussed royal pregnancy in the history of the British monarchy. The Princess of Wales, if she had thoughts of anything but her baby that night, must have breathed a heartfelt sigh of relief at the thought that she could now legitimately expect to enjoy some real privacy, a respite from the persistent speculation, criticism, advice and scrutiny which had dogged her during the past seven and a half months. It seemed a very long time since the heady days of early November 1981, when the world first learned of what in an earlier age would have been called her "interesting condition."

Like the public announcement of their engagement on 24th February 1981, and the beginning of their wedding service at St Paul's Cathedral on 29th July, the news that the Prince and Princess of Wales were expecting their first baby was released at 11 o'clock in the morning. It was Guy Fawkes Day – the 377th anniversary of the escape of King James VI and I from possible death as he opened Parliament on 5th November 1605. It was also barely three months since the Prince and Princess of Wales had married, and apart from the position of the hands on the clock as the announcement was made, there was nothing eleventh-hour about the timing of the bulletin. Anxious to thwart any attempt by the ever-vigilant Press to jump the gun, Buckingham Palace were clearly in no mood to be led by the nose into making an announcement which would merely confirm what everyone else would have been saying or suspecting

(Below right) The christening of Prince William, the child of Prince Charles and the Princess of Wales took place at Buckingham Palace. The child, born on June 21, is second in succession to the Throne and when he becomes king he will be 42nd monarch since the Norman Conquest.
(Below) The Queen and Prince Charles flank the Queen Mother as she holds her great grandson, Prince William of Wales after the ceremony today. It was also the Queen Mother's 82nd birthday.

for weeks or months. The lesson of the long, public courtship had been well and truly learned – so well, indeed, that when the news of the Princess' pregnancy eventually broke everybody confessed themselves completely taken by surprise. Crowds, mostly tourists, outside Buckingham Palace that day could not collect their thoughts sufficiently quickly to make any coherent response to the questions put to them by television reporters, and many of those approached cast a disbelieving eye about them as they suspected some novel

(Below) The Princess of Wales looks down at her son, Prince William of Wales as he sucks her little finger after the Christening Service at Buckingham Palace.

brand of television humour after the fashion of "Candid Camera" or "Game For A Laugh."

But there was no uncertainty among the much vaster crowds of London's office workers assembled along the approaches to Guildhall, where the royal couple were to attend a luncheon given by the Lord Mayor. Conceived as the City's appreciation for the choice of St Paul's as the venue for the wedding, the event turned into one of congratulation at the prospect of a second heir in direct line of succession to the Throne. And Prince Charles made unapologetic use of the occasion to pay tribute to the new mother-to-be, while those who heard him talk of "the wonderful effect my wife has had upon everyone" were not slow to comment with a wink and a nudge that she had obviously had quite an effect on him!

There was universal public delight at the news – a national

(Above) Toby Hayward and Katie Harrison rushed forward with gifts for the Queen Mother on her 82nd birthday pictured here at Clarence House before the Christening.
(Right) The Princess of Wales holds Prince William after the Christening flanked by the Queen and the Queen Mother. Prince Charles and the Duke of Edinburgh stand behind them.

reflection of the private reaction of the two families most closely involved. The Royal Family's response was delivered second-hand by Press Secretaries who shared out the traditional epithets "thrilled," "delighted," "pleased" etc without further comment. Lord Spencer, speaking from his holiday home in Brighton, felt able to expand. "I can't say how happy we are," he said. "Diana wanted this child. She loves young people and they adore her. She will be a marvellous mother." The following day's newspapers took up where the families left off and, armed with facts and figures speculatively accumulated for three months against the eventuality, regaled their readers with the minutiae traditional to such occasions. Two of the most obvious causes of comment and even wonder were the youthfulness of the

Princess and the speed with which she had conceived. It was in fact almost 120 years since a Princess of Wales or future Queen had been so young with child or at such a short interval after marriage – that was Princess Alexandra, the wife of the future King Edward VII. She was barely nineteen when in January 1864 she gave birth to Prince Albert Victor, the ill-fated elder brother of King George V. And, like her mother-in-law Queen Victoria she produced less than ten months after her marriage – though in fairness to any reputations the family may wish to maintain each was some weeks premature!

Unlike many of the pregnancies of those early Victorian times, there was never any serious doubt that the pregnancy that would produce 1982's royal baby would be a thoroughly healthy one. Antenatal care would be available at the touch of a button, dispensed under the practised eye of Mr George Pinker, who had brought no fewer than seven royal infants into the world in as many years. There were no appreciable gynaecological difficulties in the history of

The Queen with her youngest child, Prince Edward, in 1964 (below). Prince Andrew, when four, holds his baby brother (right).

either the Princess' own family, where only the death in 1960 of her brother John, who survived birth for less than twenty-four hours, cast a shadow over the prospects, or in the Royal Family itself. The Princess' appreciation of children, well-publicised by scores of photographs of her holding babies, guiding toddlers, talking to schoolchildren and comparing notes with young mothers, made Lord Spencer's remarks totally credible. Few doubted that she would have an early family and many now think she will have a large one. Her involvement was fortified in February 1982 when she became Patron of five organisations, of which four were charities established for the benefit of various groups of children. With her fresh-air approach to

Mothers and babies. (Below) Princess Alexandra with her son James Ogilvy in 1964, and Princess Anne with her son Peter Phillips in 1978. (Left) Christening day for Master Peter in 1977, for Lord Frederick Windsor in July 1979, and (bottom picture) for the Earl of Ulster, born in October 1974.

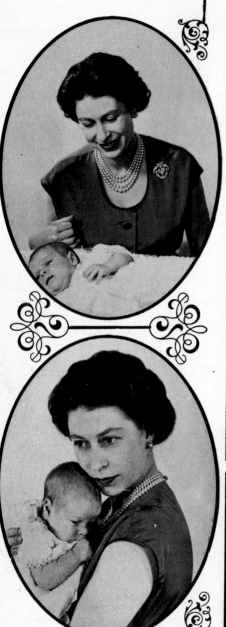

Cecil Beaton's portraits (below) of the Queen with Prince Andrew in March 1960.

life, and the wholesale breaking of the old rules of royal pregnancies, she was set for a happy and confident time and an experience which her future subjects could visibly share with her.

In the long term this was how it turned out, though in the ensuing months there were difficulties which she may not have anticipated and which cast the odd cloud over her own radiance and

(Right) The widowed Princess Marina with her three children in 1943 and (above) the Queen Mother with her three grandchildren in 1960. (Opposite) The Princess of Wales.

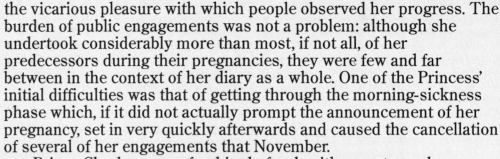

the vicarious pleasure with which people observed her progress. The burden of public engagements was not a problem: although she undertook considerably more than most, if not all, of her predecessors during their pregnancies, they were few and far between in the context of her diary as a whole. One of the Princess' initial difficulties was that of getting through the morning-sickness phase which, if it did not actually prompt the announcement of her pregnancy, set in very quickly afterwards and caused the cancellation of several of her engagements that November.

Prince Charles was refreshingly frank with reporters who clamoured for a statement of the obvious: he told them they all had wives and must know the problems. On one occasion at Bristol he apologised to his audience for not being able to bring his wife, and cheerfully accepted all responsibility for her condition. But despite an attempt to fulfil some later engagements, the indisposition seemed to go on and on. "Nobody ever told me it would be as bad as this," complained the Princess at Chesterfield – and as less and less was seen of her right up to Christmas, it did seem as if she was suffering more prolonged and severe bouts than normal and was powerless to shake them off. By mid-January, Buckingham Palace was able to confirm that she was now "perfectly well except for the odd indisposition caused by her pregnancy" and to promise that she would undertake a programme of engagements until early in April,

(Below) The Princess of Wales sitting in her pram at Park House Sandringham in 1963. Eventually she took charge of toddlers (below right) at the Young England Kindergarten at Pimlico.

(Opposite page) Diana after her engagement, photographed by Snowdon, 1981.

and probably beyond. "The Princess," came the assurance, "wants to carry out engagements for as long as she feels able and well enough."

For a short time the threat existed that she might not be well enough for much longer. Princess Michael of Kent let slip a remark that her cousin was going through an obsession for strict dieting, as an antidote to the inevitable process of weight-gaining which accompanies advancing pregnancy and involves an addition to normal body weight of up to 24 lbs. Overwhelming advice flooded in from all quarters in a well-meant attempt to save the Princess from

imminent extinction. Eating for two was loudly praised, though the more cautious specified that little and often was the watchword, with lean meat, fish, cereal and dairy products predominating over sugar and carbohydrates. This latter injunction was soon seen to be lost on the Princess who shortly afterwards was spotted nipping out of her car into a sweet shop in the Kings Road and emerging again with a fistful of sweets and chocolates – an incident gaily passed off as a forgiveable concession to her celebrated sweet tooth. There was little to support the theory that it represented a surrender to the tensions

Diana's wedding provided some of the happiest balcony scenes since the Queen's Coronation in 1953 (above right), when Prince Charles was not yet five.

to which she was supposed to have been subjected in recent weeks – overmuch publicity, tiffs with her husband, the first movements of the baby – but some sections of the Press milked it for all it was worth. She was said to be looking decidedly peaky by mid-February, but Buckingham Palace said that she was "perfectly fit and well" and would extend her programme of official engagements to take in the opening of the Albany Trust's centre at Deptford as far ahead, and as close to the expected birth, as the middle of May.

The newshounds were on the scent again when in March the Princess accompanied Prince Charles to Cheltenham for an afternoon's racing on Gold Cup Day. Here she seemed to experience one of those unexplained black moods of which she had long been suspected and which had contributed to the image of a woman with her own uncompromising set of likes and dislikes. Either she had not wanted to go to the races that day, or the weather was too cold for her, or there were deeper problems that onlookers could only

After a fortnight's Mediterranean cruise, the royal couple spent ten happy and restful weeks at Balmoral.

the revelation that the couple would spend part of April holidaying at the Prince's cottage "Tamarisk" on the Isles of Scilly. The prospect thrilled the Scillonians and seemed to improve the Princess' temperament immediately. It also left everyone wondering about her deterioration in the first place, and commentators were kept busy piecing together a jigsaw of possibilities which included the pressures of moving house, the difficulty of adjusting to her new role, the preoccupation with security and the intrusions into her privacy. It might have been as well simply to pass it all off as the sort of temporary depression or mild nervous fatigue invariably connected with pregnancy from time to time – an explanation which, in the light of the unremitting good health and spirits enjoyed by the Princess in the last two months before her confinement, is probably as good and sufficient as any. Her engagements tailed off, and her public sightings were confined to the polo fields of Ham, Windsor and the New Forest where she was seen in the full bloom of approaching motherhood and where there was no mistaking her evident enjoyment of life.

As royal pregnancies go this was a pleasantly light-hearted affair in which the main protagonists made no unnecessary secret of their delighted reactions to the prospect of parenthood, while public discussion was on the whole sensible and informative. It is quite astonishing to find so little being said publicly about royal confinements even as recently as the 1920's, when it was still an indispensible part of social life to be able to read between the lines if a member of the Royal family was "indisposed" or "out of town." Much of the protective veil of secrecy which so ineffectively concealed the truth owed its origin to the taboos of the Victorian age which Queen Victoria, so forward-looking and prejudice-free in many surprising respects, did little to discourage. Where childbirth was concerned,

she was implacably hostile right from the start – an attitude derived from her own dislike of the process. Even on the night before her wedding in 1840, she was openly confessing her dread of having children, and soon after the birth of her first child she wrote to her uncle, King Leopold I of the Belgians: "I think, dearest uncle, you

cannot really wish me to be the 'Mamma d'une nombreuse famille'…Men never think what a hard task it is for us women to go through this very often." Indeed she was frequently secretly enraged against her husband Prince Albert for no more compelling reason than that he was exempt from the strains and inconvenience of producing children. "What made me so miserable," she wrote to her daughter in 1858, "was to have the first two years of my married life utterly spoilt by this occupation. I could enjoy nothing." It didn't stop her from having no fewer than nine children, but even so she could find no pleasure in it save for the possible consolation of doing her duty. Thinking of England, they call it nowadays.

Nor could Queen Victoria share other people's enjoyment of their pregnancies. When her eldest daughter announced to her that she

was expecting her first child – the future Kaiser Wilhelm II – she greeted the news as "horrid," and wrote: "What you say of the pride of giving life to an immortal soul is very fine, dear, but I own I cannot enter into that: I think much more of our being like a cow or a dog at such moments, when our poor nature becomes so animal and unecstatic." This open and unswervable aversion did not, however, dissuade her from dispensing advice and enquiring after details in regard to members of her family who were expecting children. In later life her reputation for match-making was rivalled by her delight in forecasting birth-dates. "I understand the last time you were *unwell* ended on 17th May," she confided to her granddaughter Princess Victoria of Hesse. "This led me to calculate that the event should take place between 20th and 27th February…" "Don't ride too much," she advised on another occasion, "and above all if you were not regular in other respects." Long accounts of the birth of her youngest daughter Beatrice's first baby in 1886 were laced with generous descriptions of the father's delighted reactions. In 1891 she conducted her own episolatory post-mortem on the death in childbed

46

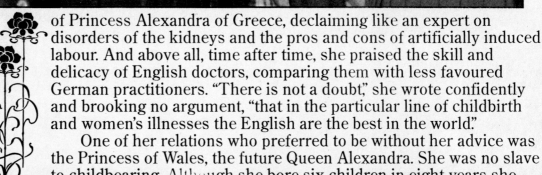

of Princess Alexandra of Greece, declaiming like an expert on disorders of the kidneys and the pros and cons of artificially induced labour. And above all, time after time, she praised the skill and delicacy of English doctors, comparing them with less favoured German practitioners. "There is not a doubt," she wrote confidently and brooking no argument, "that in the particular line of childbirth and women's illnesses the English are the best in the world."

One of her relations who preferred to be without her advice was the Princess of Wales, the future Queen Alexandra. She was no slave to childbearing. Although she bore six children in eight years she

Conversation and contentment at Queensferry, and a kiss for Lord Snowdon at Caernarvon Castle.

never allowed pregnancy to come between her and her whirling social life – a fact which Queen Victoria deeply deplored. It is possible that the Queen's unconcealed disapproval of the "fast" life which she and the Prince of Wales led explained why she was never encouraged to be present in the same house whenever any of the Princess' children were born. The first child was born almost two months prematurely – indeed nothing was ready save a robe, a basket, eight yards of flannel and a sheet of wadding, and the Princess' companion Lady Macclesfield had to use her own petticoat as a receiving flannel. The second son also arrived before time and Queen Victoria, deprived on two successive occasions of seeing her senior grandchildren born, began to wonder whether Princess Alexandra wasn't deliberately over-estimating the term of her pregnancies in order to mislead her – a suspicion more than justified by the continual conflict between them over how to bring the children up.

Variations in Welsh weather: chilly for a nostalgic return to Caernarvon (opposite page), fine and breezy at St David's next day (right), with a downpour at Carmarthen later (above).

If anything, Queen Mary, the wife of King George V, was inclined to share Queen Victoria's feelings on the subject. A reserved, easily embarrassed character, she opened her heart to her favourite aunt, the Grand Duchess of Mecklenburg-Strelitz: "Having babies is highly distasteful to me," she wrote just after the birth of her third son in 1900, "though when once they are there they are very nice!" Like Queen Victoria, she was distressed at being helplessly idle during pregnancy – another consequence of the tight social code of the time, and she made almost identical complaints. "This is, alas, the penalty of being a woman," she wrote plaintively to her husband. Above all she dreaded being conspicuous in the later months – an understandable emotion in those days when wasp-waists were *de rigueur*. "She does not wish it remarked or mentioned," warned the Princess Royal in 1897, with evident disdain for her outwardly unmaternal instincts.

The much more breezy social atmosphere in Britain after the Great War brought with it a gradual, though reluctant, relaxation in the royal approach to childbirth and to the public treatment of it –

both Princess Mary's pregnancies in 1922 and 1924, and the Duchess of York's in 1925 and 1930 were commented on comparatively freely and in good taste while they were in progress. But it was still rare for royal ladies to be seen visibly pregnant in public, and it was not until the 1960's that the attitude and practice noticeably changed. Late in 1961, Princess Margaret, then expecting her first baby, was frequently out and about -- though not on public engagements -- and on one occasion was photographed at the opera wearing a long, maternity

South Wales saw the Princess at her most stylish and beautiful on 29th October

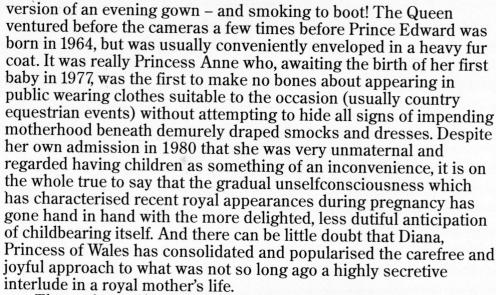

version of an evening gown – and smoking to boot! The Queen ventured before the cameras a few times before Prince Edward was born in 1964, but was usually conveniently enveloped in a heavy fur coat. It was really Princess Anne who, awaiting the birth of her first baby in 1977, was the first to make no bones about appearing in public wearing clothes suitable to the occasion (usually country equestrian events) without attempting to hide all signs of impending motherhood beneath demurely draped smocks and dresses. Despite her own admission in 1980 that she was very unmaternal and regarded having children as something of an inconvenience, it is on the whole true to say that the gradual unselfconsciousness which has characterised recent royal appearances during pregnancy has gone hand in hand with the more delighted, less dutiful anticipation of childbearing itself. And there can be little doubt that Diana, Princess of Wales has consolidated and popularised the carefree and joyful approach to what was not so long ago a highly secretive interlude in a royal mother's life.

That welcome development has been reflected in the sincerity of the public response to royal mothers-to-be, and in the case of the

present Princess of Wales the traditional, unwritten rule of distance between royalty and its public has been bridged so substantially as to allow that response to be made very positively. Consequently one of the commonest sights associated with her during her pregnancy was that of her receiving some gift of clothes or toys from one or other member of the public – usually a child – in the course of her

That final day in Wales took the couple from Builth to Newport, including Llwynypia Hospital where they spoke to nursing and expectant mothers. A week later, Diana announced her own good news.

engagements. Once the fashion caught on it became impossible to stop: from teddy bears in Brixton to knitted layettes in Leeds, presents for the forthcoming baby were thrust towards the Princess with unrelenting generosity. By February Prince Charles was commenting with amazement on the "thousands" of cardigans, pairs of bootees and "knickers of all kinds" which he and his wife had received for their baby. In March, the Royal Wedding Gifts Office at Buckingham Palace was closed down after eight months of dealing with presents valued at over eleven million pounds, but it became immediately necessary to set up a similar office to cope with and carefully record the rush of baby offerings. By the end of May almost two thousand gifts had been received at Buckingham Palace, Highgrove House and Kensington Palace. The Princess saw and inspected every one, and helped to decide which of the many duplicates should be sent on to orphanages and hospitals.

Some gifts were presented on formal occasions to the royal

couple personally, like the high-chair, hand-made in cleft oak by Richard la Trobe Bateman, and given to Prince Charles when he opened the Craft Council's Gallery in London in February. The Prince enquired about how it had been tested: "Has a child sat on it, or just someone with a very small bottom?" Other presents came from less likely sources: an imaginative editor of a German weekly magazine

guards, resourceful operators – crowded into boats or lying in wait behind bushes – found sufficient opportunities to obtain their pictures.

The publication of the pictures, in particular one of the Princess demonstrably pregnant and wearing a bikini, infuriated the Queen,

whose Press Secretary Michael Shea deplored them as being "in the worst possible taste. It is apparent that these pictures were taken without the Prince and Princess being aware of this. Such tasteless behaviour is in breach of the normally accepted British Press standards in respect of the privacy of individuals." The royal protest was not unique: the switchboard at Buckingham Palace was jammed by calls from loyal subjects, MP's signed motions in the House of Commons attacking both papers and regretting that their editors "should have fallen so far short of the professional standards of journalism," the Press Council started an investigation, Fleet Street in general disapproved, the *Daily Express* making a particular display of

sanctimonious dissociation, and the offending editors prepared to throw in the towel. One newspaper executive, however, decried the fuss which everyone was so obviously enjoying, and was disgusted at the two offenders for not making a fight of it. As if to acknowledge his point, they both gave in only with a final touch of defiant mischief. *The Sun* published its apology accompanied by one of the very pictures that had caused the rumpus in the first place, and protested that the photographs "brought a breath of summer into the lives of millions of our readers back in chilly Britain. Of course it was never our intention to offend. If we have done so then we are deeply sorry. But we still think that Princess Di looks terrific." This

transparently tongue-in-cheek assurance was mirrored by *The Sun's* partner-in-crime, of whom it could fairly be said that the lady doth protest too much. "We published out of deep affection," said the *Daily Star*, wide-eyed with outraged innocence. "We were pleased to see Diana enjoying herself and thought our readers would want to share her joy, especially as many of them had telephoned us saying how tired she had looked on TV the night before. We felt the British public would want to know that Diana was looking so well and lovely." Behind the smokescreen of words, both papers withdrew their photographers from the island, promised to leave the royal couple in peace and declared that they would not now be selling the rights to reproduce their pictures to potential customers. The excitement melted away almost as quickly as it had arisen.

Other issues soon took its place however. Foremost among them in terms of a significance which, in the light of events, became less obvious was the question of the baby's sex. It was indeed as well that Prince William was born a boy, for the fact swept under the red carpet a question that threatened to exercise the minds of all manner

Happy return from Eleuthera in February: Charles and Diana after their ten-day holiday with the Romseys. Press intrusion had once threatened its success.

of folk, from Members of Parliament to the humblest provincial branches of Women's Rights movements. The dreaded law of male primogeniture, by which the succession to the Throne falls to the sons of the sovereign before daughters, acknowledging the priority of older children only within this male-preferred structure, raised its ugly head as soon as the sex of the unborn child graduated from mere sentimental curiosity to a matter of constitutional principle in an increasingly egalitarian society.

Changing fashion for a Princess. A breezy look at Cheltenham in March 1981 and at Windsor in June contrasts with the warm cape at York in November.

For some years now the concept – age-old in the annals of the British monarchy and strengthened by ratification in the Act of Settlement of 1701 – has come under growing criticism as being contrary to the spirit, if not to the letter, of various pieces of Parliamentary legislation passed in recent times to give women

1938 when her mother, by then Queen Consort, was rumoured to be pregnant again. Officially, of course, the Queen's views are unavailable and, constitutionally correct as she has always been, she would not on the grounds of personal distaste alone have withheld the Royal Assent to any reforming Bill presented to her. In the event the

Bill's first attempt foundered for want of Government time, although a second reading was booked for early July, and the opinion gained ground that the Prime Ministers of the seventeen Commonwealth countries would not have agreed to the change, which would have affected their own Head of State as well as Britain's.

The argument proved too much for Earl Spencer who, when asked about his personal preferences for a grandchild, said: "I hope it's a boy. It would solve any problems." The bookmakers reflected

All at ease as the Princess of Wales meets the queen of Hollywood. Elizabeth Taylor starred in the play "The Little Foxes" which opened on 8th March at London's Victoria Palace Theatre. Diana attended the charity première—another of her increasing number of solo engagements. Both celebrities confessed to a dream come true— each had always wanted to meet the other.

that hope: they were offering 11-10 on a boy, evens for a girl and 20-1 against twins – hardly attractive odds for serious business, but then the chances never offer much scope. (It was interesting that the odds against twins had been reduced from 50-1 to 20-1 by the beginning of the New Year. Though twins have been an extreme rarity in the Royal Family, and result from only one pregnancy in eighty generally, the Spencer and Fermoy family trees show that the Princess of Wales is only two and three generations removed from ancestors who were themselves twins, and that there are two sets of twins among her immediate cousins.)

By the middle of April *The Observer*, rarely prone to indulge itself in speculation of this type, revealed that the Princess had recently undergone an ultra-scan which showed, among other things, that she was carrying a boy. Buckingham Palace remained resolutely tight-

Tea and concern: Diana in March, during her visit to Huddersfield to meet disadvantaged social groups.

Elizabeth and Edward – after his death in 1547. Behind all these machinations lay Henry VIII's obsession with ensuring the direct succession to the Throne in the male line. The repeated failure of his first wife Katharine of Aragon to produce surviving male progeny led him to seek a second wife in Anne Boleyn – a move which entailed the breach with Rome – and her failure to give him a son prompted him to have her executed on the grounds of infidelity and to marry Jane Seymour, the eventual mother of Edward VI. The fusion of politics with religion gave the rivalries added point – Mary had been brought up a Catholic and had been declared illegitimate; Elizabeth,

an avowed Protestant, had been imprisoned; Edward, their younger brother, represented the only male Protestant hope of England, but at nine years old was the mere puppet of his two so-called Protectors, the Earls of Somerset and Northumberland. It was Northumberland who placed his own daughter-in-law Lady Jane Grey on the Throne on Edward's death in 1553. Mary replaced her after less than a fortnight and then faced five years of intrigue while supporters of her half-sister Elizabeth contrived to reinstate the Protestant faith.

It says much for the development of Britain's constitutional monarchy and Parliamentary democracy that the sex of the heir to the Throne has never since assumed the significance of those Machiavellian days. The lack of an obvious male heir has frequently been inconvenient, but the background and preferences of heirs presumptive or apparent have featured much more strongly.

The succession question in Elizabeth I's day was a perennial headache to the Queen's courtiers as well as to the Queen herself and her ultimate, almost resigned, choice of James VI of Scotland led to the constant religious turmoils of the early seventeenth century, as

Diana returns from ...eds after opening St Gemm... Hospice, where she revealed t... ...he was expecting her baby on ...t July. She was ten d...rs out.

both James and his son Charles I attempted to reconcile their Roman Catholic upbringing and inclinations with the increasingly Puritanical demands of a strong and determined Parliament. A later Parliament opted to dispense with the possibility of a repetition of those turmoils when James II was deposed in 1688 and his Catholic son debarred from the succession in favour of the King's overtly Protestant daughter Mary II, and her equally Protestant husband William of Orange. Problems of a successor to Queen Anne, childless after the death of her last surviving son – another Prince William – in 1700, were despatched by the Act of Settlement the following year, by which the Crown devolved ultimately to the Elector of Hanover, a great-grandson of James I and a Protestant sovereign in his own right.

There has never been any constitutional doubt about the succession to the Throne since Queen Anne's death in 1702, but in 1817 the almost unthinkable prospect emerged whereby none of King George III's large family of fifteen children would produce a living heir capable of succeeding them. The panic arose when, in November of that year, Princess Charlotte, the only child of the Prince of Wales, died giving birth to a stillborn son. This dynastic catastrophe left the nation not only in deep mourning but also with the unsavoury probability of a succession of ageing and discreditable brothers following their ailing old father onto the Throne of Britain, without any hope or promise of a respite in the form of a vigorous, forward-

The Mountbatten connection. (Top) Lord Mountbatten at Broadlands and (above) his grandson with Diana in May 1981. (Top right) Diana with the Queen Mother and Princess Margaret at a society wedding in May 1981.

looking representative of a younger generation. This in turn led to an even less picturesque royal stampede among those profligate and self-seeking brothers as they forsook their mistresses and searched royal Europe to find wives and beget children. Within eight months the only three bachelor princes had married, and within a further ten months all, miraculously, had fathered children. The eldest of these instant fathers later became King William IV but both of his legitimate children predeceased him. Of the two other contenders Edward Duke of Kent, who was next in line after William, produced the daughter who survived them both and maintained her supreme and indisputable claim to the Throne. She succeeded in 1837 as Queen Victoria and thereafter the succession to the Throne ceased to be a bone of contention of any kind.

How far the Princess of Wales let the weight of history intrude upon her own pregnancy can well be imagined. Prince Charles may have been fascinated by the stories of the past and the contrasts and parallels they offer, but his wife was meanwhile losing no time concerning herself with the present and making sure that the nurseries at Kensington Palace and Highgrove House were properly kitted out in time for the baby's arrival. Late in January she ordered some £400 worth of nursery furniture – a chest of drawers, a toy-box, a table and a chair – from the oddly-named shop "Dragons," in Walton Street, Chelsea. The furniture was not particularly exclusive, except for the attractive – if rather twee – touch of red, white and blue cotton-tail rabbits romping merrily all over it and tugging at balloons – for once not the blue and silver affairs which dominated the Royal Wedding. These decorative extras were lovingly hand-painted by one of the shop's assistants, Penny Streeter, though the concept of combining the patriotic colours with the story-book whimsy may

well have been someone else's. At all events, the idea has full royal approval and the furniture now stands in the pale blue-and-pink-walled nurseries – bi-coloured to cover the possibility of a boy or a girl – at Kensington Palace.

Into those newly-designed chests and boxes will go the massive quantity of baby clothes which the Princess has been acquiring steadily for her son over the months. Many of these will have come from members of her admiring public, but as she is well known to have her own ideas on baby fashion and will, as every mother does, want to experiment, the bulk of the clothes are of her own choice. Like her sister-in-law Princess Anne, she has relied heavily upon Harrod's for her purchases – she made several personal visits there in the last few weeks before her confinement – but an even

more exclusive source of supply came from the New Bond Street baby boutique "Please Mum." Its director, Gilbert Frankel, and his brother Philip have been in the business for four years and now run four branches in London. Their stock of clothes is highly acclaimed and highly-priced – romper suits can be as expensive as £70 – but the designing is of the most prestigious calibre. All the garments are made abroad, and only the best known European designers, including Pierre Cardin, are represented.

In contrast, the royal nurseries may have to take in the

Diana was in great form at Liverpool on 2nd April, when she attended the opening of a pagoda-style centre for members of the 10,000-strong Chinese community of Merseyside.

occasional family favourite in terms of furniture, foremost among which is the 140-year-old cast-iron cradle which has rocked royal babies since the marriage of Queen Victoria, together with an old wicker cot, all trimmed with lace and yellow ribbon. Prince William will almost certainly lie in it only once, dressed in the splendid robe of Honiton lace made for Queen Victoria's first child in 1840 – and that will be at the time of his christening and for the benefit of the Court photographer. After that the cradle may, and the robe will, be put back into storage. For outdoor use, the well-known royal pram may see the light of day for the ninth royal baby since it was given to the present Queen Mother by King George V and Queen Mary in 1926, ready for the birth of their first granddaughter. The pram has the advantage of being large and extremely well-sprung – and as carefully maintained as any carriage from the Royal Mews – while its high sides are reputed to be the perfect barrier to draughts and

Merseysiders, said it with flowers on this colourful Spring day. One toddler gave Diana a bunch of tulips, flung his arms round her neck and kissed her She, and the crowd, loved it.

fumes. Against that, and for all its august history, it is something of a museum piece – unfashionably low, ungraceful and visibly out-o date. No forward-looking nanny would wish to be seen wheeling it in Kensington Gardens, conspicuous by its vintage uniqueness amid an armada of spanking new models. Some newspaper readers were horrified to learn that its use was being considered, and one correspondent favoured its consignment to a museum rather than its "being inflicted upon the Princess of Wales." It will of course be her choice, and she may tactfully agree to its being used only in the seclusion of private gardens, while preferring a more up-to-date version for public use. All of which will be lost on the occupant as he waves his ivory-handled rattle – a gift to the Queen Mother when she was born in 1900, and passed on to Prince Charles in 1948.

And in that pram – whichever it may be – Prince William will be wheeled up and down, hundreds of miles a year, by a newcomer to royal service in the shape of Barbara Barnes. As his recently-appointed nanny, she will take charge of him for the foreseeable

future, after his initial few weeks in the care of a nursing sister. There was, up until early May – within only six weeks of the birth – intense interest in the choice of a nanny, not least because many people rather improbably believed that the absence of a public announcement meant that the Princess intended to look after the baby herself. One newspaper became openly impatient and demanded "Can't Charles and Diana agree on a Nanny?" But by all accounts the procedure was not easy: there were thousands of applications to be considered, and the nanny-vacancy grapevine was fairly buzzing with rumours and recommendations which filtered

through to friends and acquaintances of the royal household. Furthermore the choice had to be good, and good first time: the risk of prejudicing the early years of a future King had to be minimised as any mistakes could not easily be reversed.

The role of the British nanny in today's society appears at first sight to be anachronistic. Most of us have little concept of being

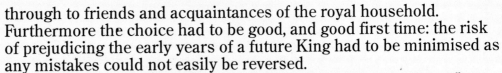

Happiness and interest at Aintree – a marked contrast to Cheltenham on Gold Cup Day when Diana seemed depressed. Now, on Grand National Day, she watched the racing from the balcony above Lord Derby's box.

Lord Snowdon's portrait of Diana (opposite) was taken in April and released on her 21st birthday.

brought up by one and are reminded that they exist at all only by the sight of one – or a gaggle of them – wheeling charges through the great parks of west London. To those for whom the word itself does not conjure up even so much as a television series or a film starring Bette Davies, the notion of a nanny is as vague and distant as the Boer War. Speculation as to the Princess of Wales' choice seemed

therefore to go as counter to the times as to the Princess' own youth and innovative outlook, yet it was never really in doubt that ultimately her endless round of public engagements and the demanding programme of tours abroad – whether she takes her son with her or not – leave her with no alternative but to employ a nanny to attend to the day-to-day requirements of his upbringing.

If there is any truth in the maxim that the hand that rocks the cradle rules the world, or in the statement, attributed to Wellington, that the Battle of Waterloo was won on the playing fields of Eton, British history must owe something of its unfolding to the British nanny, ubiquitous in aristocratic society for centuries as the intellect- and character-forming bridge between the cradle and the schoolroom. Time was when nannies were not nannies unless they had been trained at England's foremost training establishment,

Norland. It was founded in the mid-19th century and by its end was so renowned that Norland-trained nannies filled the nurseries of almost every royal household in Europe. Perversely, British royalty rarely insisted on Norland qualifications, but has nevertheless enjoyed good value for money from the succession of nannies-cum-governesses who have guarded future sovereigns since the childhood of Queen Victoria.

Indeed, the monarchy probably owes more than it cares to admit to the woman who shepherded Queen Victoria through her formative years, Baroness Lehzen. "A clever, agreeable woman," according to the diarist Charles Greville, she assumed responsibility for the young princess from the age of five, though she had already made a

Charles and Diana were part of an 80,000 Aintree crowd. For the Grand National itself they travelled to the Canal Turn to watch the race at close quarters. As the horses approached they clambered onto their Land Rover for a better view.

With the royal couple was Mrs Nick Gaselee (in white hat), the wife of Charles' National Hunt trainer, and the mother of one of Diana's bridesmaids.

favourable impression as an occasional nurse, taking Victoria for walks and reading to her while she was being dressed. Her strict outlook and strength of character eventually wore down even Princess Victoria's petulant Hanoverian temper so that long before her accession in 1837 her charge had developed the greatest affection for her. Utterly discreet to the end, Lehzen fell victim to one of those notorious intrigues which seemed to plague Queen

Another day in Wales. Diana opened a Sony TV factory at Bridgend on 7th April. The headgear was for safety—and publicity.

Victoria's early Court, but long after the Baroness' death her loyalty and devotion was openly praised by the Queen, who knew her debt to the woman who first prompted her to promise "I will be good."

Queen Victoria's choice of nurse for her children was no less happy and, in events which she did not live to see but would warmly

have appreciated, appropriate. For she chose the widowed Sarah, Lady Lyttleton, a daughter of the 2nd Earl Spencer, and a woman of such humility that it was difficult to persuade her into service at all. When she took the post as governess to the infant Princess Royal she found she was a natural for it. She was devout, reflecting the Queen's own moral outlook; cultivated, satisfying the requirement

Prince Albert had laid down; and had an apt sense of humour, which went down well with the Princess Royal herself. As "Laddle" and "Princessy" they became firm and lasting friends. But Lady Lyttleton's attitude toward the heir to the Throne, Albert Edward, Prince of Wales, is much more interesting: like his mother before him "Bertie" had an infamous temper, but Lady Lyttleton very nearly cured him of it, replacing his "passions and stampings" with a sense of human dignity and almost programmed politeness. Her genuine affection for him, combined with a sense of proportion which was at times sadly absent in his parents, fired his devotion for her. She in her turn was able to discover in him an intelligence which, because of his laziness, his parents later ceased to believe in, and to initiate a sympathetic course of education which unfortunately did not survive the rigours of the Prince Consort's subsequent régime.

The heyday of the royal nanny in the 19th century seems to have proved benign and constructive for the children, though the fashion for childish nicknames sometimes got out of hand. Princess Alice, later Countess of Athlone, much admired her nanny Jane Potts but her name lent itself to the soubriquet "Cow Patt" – though if the origin of the name is obscure the sentiment behind it might be traced to the Princess' Uncle Bertie, who found the woman unattractive and

called her "Mademoiselle Vase." Nevertheless she was, according to the Princess, wise, kind and interesting, taking her for long, delightful walks and inculcating a deep and vivid sense of history by encouraging her and her brother to act out Roman battles and scenes from everyday life in ancient Greece.

The children of King George V and Queen Mary – particularly the two eldest – were not so lucky. Prince Edward, later Duke of Windsor, was plagued by a nurse whose possessiveness impelled her to pinch and twist his arm just before he was brought in to see his parents each afternoon. They took his state of loud and uncontrollable distress for ill-temper and sent him straight back to his nurse, without attempting to enquire further. The nurse was also responsible for mistreating his brother – later King George VI – and

On doctor's orders, Diana took a 4-day break towards the end of April in the Scilly Isles—part of the Duchy of Cornwall. This was her first visit, though Charles had been there twice before. On the evening of their arrival they went into the centre of St Mary's to meet the locals.

her habit of bottle-feeding him during bumpy carriage-rides is said to explain the stomach disorders which dogged him all his life. It was only when she suffered a nervous breakdown that the truth emerged and she was replaced by Mrs Bill. This was a merciful substitution. Efficient, and above all humane, "Lalla" Bill showed a genuine concern for the health of the younger brother as well as for his sister's chest complaint; and when the later additions to the family were put under her charge she was quick to size up their qualities and failings.

Consequently King George VI in particular enjoyed a benevolent

upbringing, and this was mirrored by that of his future wife, Lady Elizabeth Bowes-Lyon. From her earliest years she and her devoted brother David were under the daily care of Clara Cooper-Knight, the daughter of a tenant on one of the many Strathmore estates. Known as "Allah" she had been nurse to all of Lady Elizabeth's seven brothers and sisters, one of whom, Lady Elphinstone, employed her to bring up her children as well. Subsequently she became nanny to the present Queen and Princess Margaret, a task she executed with supreme confidence, until 1943. In those seventeen years her calm, no-nonsense approach taught them above all to think of others. She had tried to teach the baby Princess Elizabeth to say "Mother" in time for her parents' return from Australasia in June 1927 and, more successfully, instilled an unselfish attitude into her in preparation for the birth of her younger sister in 1930. She never rammed learning into unwilling heads, but the lessons of regular nursery routine became invaluable when adjustments had to be made at the time of the Abdication and at the outbreak of War. The young princesses even had to present themselves correctly dressed before they were allowed into the air-raid shelter!

The St Mary's walkabout was a tremendous crowd puller. It took the royal couple 22 minutes to walk a hundred yards, and Diana received no fewer than 74 posies.

Mrs Knight also trained the Queen's most admired nanny, Margaret "Bobo" MacDonald. Bobo, the daughter of a Scottish gardener and coachman, actually shared a bedroom with Princess Elizabeth, and her sister Ruby became her special nursemaid after Princess Margaret was born. In later years, Bobo became Princess Elizabeth's closest confidante and as her dresser after her accession

Charles and Diana spent most of their second day visiting Tresco by private boat. The island had been closed to the public and the royal couple were able to visit, in comparative peace, its Abbey and the famous sub-tropical gardens. Here the tamarisk, which gives its name to Charles' cottage on St Mary's, grows in abundance.

she enjoyed a unique position of trust until her retirement in the 1970's. In 1932 she had been joined by Marion Crawford, who had been a teacher as well as a governess to the children of another Strathmore daughter, Lady Rose Leveson-Gower. Owing to her conscientiousness and skilful handling of Princesses Elizabeth and

Margaret, she was given a free hand by their parents, whose confidence in her was unshakeable. She repaid this by her great sense of fun and indisputable guidance and friendship towards the Princesses, though she later blotted her copybook by publishing her experiences in detail.

The most recent royal nannies of note were those responsible for bringing up Prince Charles and Princess Anne. Scottish-born Helen Lightbody, who had been nanny to Princes William and Richard of Gloucester in the mid-1940's, came into Princess Elizabeth's employment in 1948 after the birth of Prince Charles. A stickler for formality, she taught him, and later his sister, all the rudiments of correct behaviour – including those aspects where being royal involved an extra flourish. Although the children found her fairly strict, and not too easy-going, she impressed them sufficiently with her kindness to prompt Prince Charles to make a detour on one of his engagements in 1971 to visit her. She had retired in 1956, leaving

Charles takes to his boat on their second day in the Scillies, and (opposite page) Diana joins him.

Catherine Peebles and Mabel Anderson in charge of the royal children. Miss Peebles herself left shortly afterwards and it is Miss Anderson who, in royal service for 33 years, has become synonymous with the upbringing of today's princes. She has been nanny to all the Queen's children, following Miss Lightbody's stiffish example with great confidence and a welcome breath of fresh air. She combined quiet discipline with maternal concern, and brooked no straying from the paths of self-help and orderliness. Princess Anne

is said to have referred to her, rather sulkily, as Masterful Mabel after having been ticked off for not clearing up her playroom, but was in no doubt about recalling her to look after her own son Peter after his birth in 1977. Miss Anderson left Princess Anne's service in June 1981, after a reported difference of opinion between them could not be satisfactorily resolved.

Barbara Barnes, whose appointment by the Princess of Wales was announced on 9th May 1982, has all the makings of a worthy successor to the best of them. At 39, she is not so young as to be feckless or lost for ideas, and not so old as to be staid or resistant to some of the more novel suggestions which the Princess will undoubtedly wish to put into action. Refreshingly, she was not overawed by the prospect of guiding a possible future sovereign through childhood: "I treat all children as individuals. I don't see any different problem in bringing up a royal baby."

The aptness of the choice must be judged in the light of the next few years, but the indications are promising. No formal training, no Norland, no theoretical prejudices. A widish background – she has worked in France and Switzerland, as well as having had previous jobs in this country – and a healthy testimonial from her own schooldays when, at Fakenham Grammar School in Norfolk, she combined hard work and study with excellence in athletics and tennis. She was last employed by Lady Anne Tennant, a lady-in-waiting to Princess Margaret, and it was through her recommendation that Buckingham Palace was first alerted. For Lady Anne's money, Barbara was a winner, with her wonderful temperament and

patience: "I am sure Charles and Diana will find her a complete natural. She has a magical touch." A paragon of virtue too: she never smacks a child, rarely raises her voice in anger, is always courteous and charming herself, and insists on good manners in her charges. At the same time she prides herself on her sense of humour, and likes to take every opportunity of getting out into the fresh air. Most important of all, she is highly thought of by her employers and by their children, who were on first-name terms with her (as Prince William will be), and who adored her. And her horror at the suggestion that she might take to wearing uniform is a good omen for the most relaxed of modern royal nurseries. Uniform, though rapidly going out of fashion for all but the most conservative of today's nannies, has always been worn by those attending royal children, and its discontinuance manifests the updating of customs within the Palace walls.

There was a stage early in the Princess' pregnancy when nobody was seriously prepared to entertain the possibility that her baby would be born anywhere other than at one of the royal residences. The fashion amongst lesser members of the Royal Family during the previous dozen or so years had been for their babies to be delivered in hospital – mainly at St Mary's – but somehow the idea of a future King first seeing the light of day in a spartan room, twelve feet square and kitted out with standard furnishings, in surroundings as unlovable as London W2, was implausible, if not faintly comic and outrageous. Even the Queen – not then in direct line of succession to the Throne – was born "at home," which for the purpose was the London residence of her mother's parents in Bruton

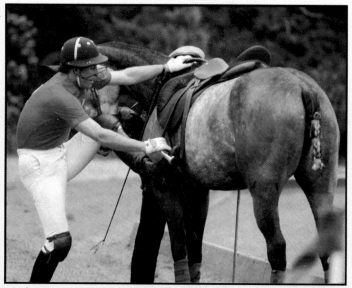

Street in fashionable Mayfair, and it was widely believed that the arrangements which had been made for the birth of each of her sons at Buckingham Palace would be repeated for the confinement of her daughter-in-law. This would have involved the conversion of the Buhl Room, with its 18th century Bavarian-style decor, into an ultra-modern confinement room with incubator, cardiotocograph, lighting and ancillary instruments and machinery, as well as the provision of comprehensive medical staffing, services and sundry facilities both before and for some time after the birth. The Queen was said to be

Diana watched Charles play polo at Windsor early in May. Her dress was a version of the previous year's Ascot dress: she wore it again when shopping at Harrod's the following June.

not only highly in favour of a Palace confinement, but also insistent upon it, pointing out that its historical significance demanded it and that the peace, quiet and total seclusion of the south side of the Palace and its familiar, homely surroundings would be beneficial to the Princess. Indeed, by April the story was about that the Buhl Room had already been converted at a cost of some £15,000.

At the same time there was a growing awareness of the practical advantages of a hospital birth – safety, scrupulous cleanliness, the immediate availability of any item of emergency equipment, well organised pre- and post-natal care. Sir John Weir, a former physician to the Queen, put the point bluntly: "Home is never as good as hospital, even if home is Buckingham Palace." The British Medical Association meanwhile had heard a tale that the Princess was

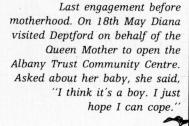

Last engagement before motherhood. On 18th May Diana visited Deptford on behalf of the Queen Mother to open the Albany Trust Community Centre. Asked about her baby, she said, "I think it's a boy. I just hope I can cope."

insisting on being confined at Buckingham Palace and protested, with just the hint of an axe to grind, that "by maintaining her position the Princess endangers her own health, that of the baby, the taxpayer's money, and throws discredit upon our hospitals." Poor Princess! Poor Queen! Even as the BMA representative spoke, arrangements were in hand for St Mary's to prepare itself for the royal arrival, and a room had already been booked – at almost £127 per day – for an admission any time from mid-June. Mr George Pinker, a man of firm persuasive qualities had, if there was ever any doubt about the issue, convinced all concerned that things would less likely be left to chance if the delivery were accomplished in hospital. And as he was the man who would – and did – perform that delivery, there was every good reason to heed his advice.

The practice of governmental representation continued unchallenged throughout the Hanoverian period, despite the virtual disappearance of any controversy surrounding the birth of potential heirs to the Throne. Queen Victoria tastefully diluted the tradition by insisting that her Home Secretary should stay discreetly in the adjoining room with the door ajar until the birth was accomplished, but the rudiments of the practice were still observed well into the twentieth century. Thus, Sir William Joynson-Hicks visited 17 Bruton

Street for the birth of the present Queen, and Mr J R Clynes went to Scotland for the birth of Princess Margaret four years later. It was then that the farcical and inconvenient side of the business was exposed. The mother-to-be had decided that her second child should be born at Glamis Castle and the birth was expected several days before it actually occurred. Mr Clynes had travelled up from London well before, in case of a premature birth, and stayed eight miles away at Airlie Castle. For fifteen days he waited, dragged endlessly to the telephone and travelling the sixteen-mile return journey every time there was a false alarm. This preposterous waste of ministerial time was not endured in vain, for as it turned out he was the last Home Secretary to have to perform this outmoded duty. When Prince Charles was expected in November 1948, King George VI decided that everyone should be spared the inconvenience and embarrassment, and the tradition passed into the sluice of history.

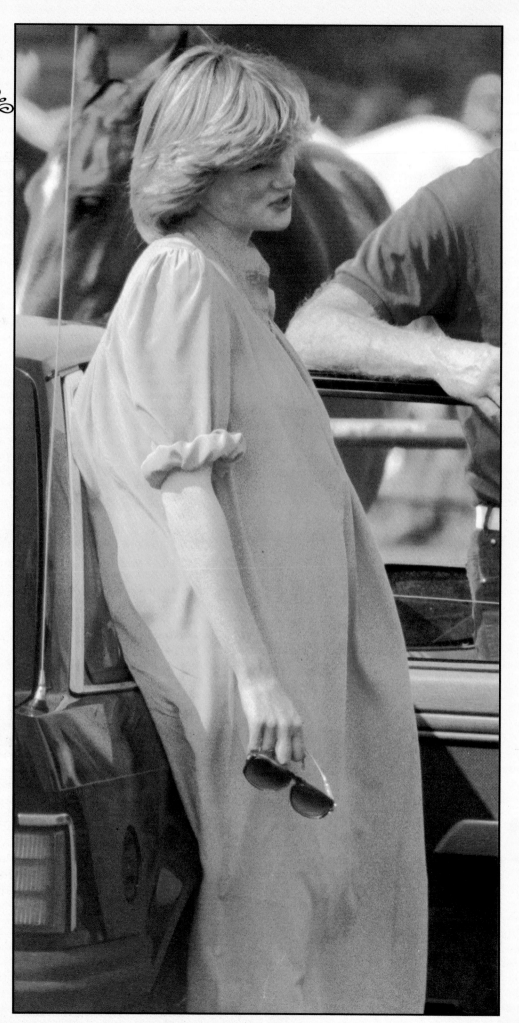

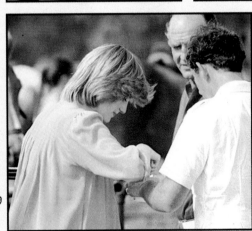

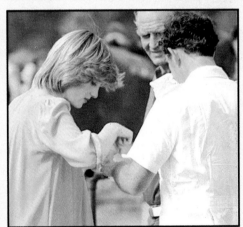

A more significant departure from the usual way in which the Royal Family governs the circumstances of the birth of its heirs was less obvious at the time. But with hindsight it is no exaggeration to say that to the British public the very thought, let alone the experience, of a Princess of Wales almost nipping into hospital, having her baby, and coming out again the following day, coupled with the open secret of her husband's close interest and involvement, and spiced with the comings and goings of their families to see the baby, was a refreshing and delightful novelty. For the crowds in the street, and those glued to radio and television sets at home, it increased the feeling of participation far beyond the hitherto rather frustrating ordeal of waiting for days outside the forbidding gates of Buckingham Palace, without any means of knowing how close the event was, for news which seemed never to arrive. The Royal Family has long since learned the art of regulating the degree of its exposure to the public, but its tacit acknowledgement that a confinement of this significance is undoubtedly an occasion for the public to be immediately informed and wholeheartedly involved was a well-timed inspiration. For the sake of maintaining the affinity between Crown and people, long may it continue.

"William is a very aristocratic name. I'm sure they had me in mind when they chose it." Willie Hamilton, MP for West Fife and the Royal Family's foremost critic and *bête noire*, was in mischievous mood on the day the new baby's names were announced. Prince William of Wales – that would be his title, said Buckingham Palace, adding hopefully that abbreviations of William were not desired – was just a week old at the time, and his father was visiting Gosport that morning. A BBC reporter decided to tackle Prince Charles on the reasons for choosing the name.

A fresh, green, polka-dot dress for Diana at Windsor the following day, when the Queen presented the Queen's Cup—but not to Les Diables Bleus, who were the beaten finalists.

"Well, what's your name?" asked the Prince.

"Nigel, sir."

"And do you know why your parents called you Nigel?" A glint of triumph in the royal eye was only fleeting: there was a reason.

"Yes, I was named after a friend of my mother's who was in the RAF."

Prince Charles paused for thought. The conversation clearly had interesting possibilities. But he decided not to take it further.

"Well, we like the name William, and it's a name that does not exist among close members of the family." His remarks paralleled those made almost sixty years earlier by his grandfather on the choice of name for the present Queen: "I hope you will approve of the names," he wrote to King George V in May 1926, "and I am sure there will be no muddle over two Elizabeths in the family. We are so anxious for her name to be Elizabeth . . . and there has been no-one of that name in your family for a long time."

Once Prince Charles' fairly terse explanation was out, it became obvious that some kind of balance had been sought between a name fit, by precedent, for a King (thus William, Henry, Stephen, John, Richard, James, Charles or George), a name by which no present member of the family is known (which eliminates all but the first

four), and a name which both the Prince and Princess of Wales liked. John was an unlikely candidate: not only was it the name of England's worst king, but it was also the name of two princes – the youngest sons of King Edward VII and of King George V – who failed to survive into adolescence, as well as of the Princess of Wales' elder brother, who died on the day of his birth in 1960. Henry sounds

irredeemably outdated, and of the other two names, Stephen has rarely enjoyed royal favour. William, the name of four previous Kings of England, one other King of Scotland and one other Duke of Normandy, was thus the choice. As chance would have it, the name is that of the baby's first cousin twice removed, Prince William of Gloucester, who was killed in a flying accident ten years ago. The name is also favoured in royal Europe, where Crown Prince Willem-Alexander of the Netherlands and Prince Guillaume of Luxemburg await their respective turns to become sovereigns – possibly contemporarily with Prince William of Wales himself. It also echoes through parts of the Princess of Wales' pedigree: though it is virtually unknown in the Spencer line, Ruth Lady Fermoy is the daughter of William Gill, while the Dukes of Devonshire, from whom both the Prince and Princess are descended, bore the name for several generations.

The baby's second name, Arthur – an unexpected choice, going

as it does very much against the current trend – has an interesting link with British history. One of the Queen's six godparents was Prince Arthur, Duke of Connaught – Queen Victoria's third son – who was himself so called after one of *his* godparents, Arthur, the great Duke of Wellington. Arthur is also one of Prince Charles' own names, as well as the only one of the new baby's names with any possible connection with Wales – via the faintest chance that King Arthur was Welsh, or at least Celtic. Neither of Prince William's final Christian names, Philip and Louis, leaves any room for doubt or ambiguity: they each celebrate the great influence which in the last half century the Mountbattens have wielded over the history of the nation, the House of Windsor and the life of Prince Charles himself.

The choice of names, inspired largely by the overpowering considerations of family tradition, may not seem startlingly imaginative, though, in fairness the feeling of anticlimax may have had a lot to do with the widespread discussion of the possibilities long before the announcement, by which time almost every probable name was a household word. Nor will the choice have by any means pleased everyone, but when the whole world tends to claim some right to be represented in a royal name, universal satisfaction is impossible without recourse to a whole string of names – like the seven borne by the Duke of Windsor, the eight borne by Queen Mary or even the 89 given to one Spanish prince – which nowadays would make a mockery of the entire business. Thus the Principality of Wales did not get David, which it was no doubt hoping for; the Spencer family was barely represented; and even Prince Charles may

The Royal Family, including Charles and Diana, acknowledge the RAF's birthday tribute after the Trooping the Colour ceremony on 12th June. (Below) The Queen and Prince Edward in earlier years.

have wanted George, as a tribute to the King he knows only in the misty and unreliable recollection of childhood – his grandfather, George VI.

It is interesting to speculate how far the Prince and Princess of Wales were influenced by close members of their families to include, or indeed to omit, certain names, though it is doubtful whether they suffered the uncomfortable pressure which Queen Victoria brought to bear on so many of her own descendants. She was obsessed by the desire, which, in its defence, she said was common to "a great many families," to have her name or that of her husband perpetuated in all her children and their issue. The instruction: "Of course, you will add Albert at the end," or: "I wish all the girls to have Victoria" intruded upon every newly confined mother, and the order was invariably and unquestioningly complied with. In addition the Queen almost supervised the selection of the other names, commenting on the parents' own choices with what today seems incredible forthrightness. "I fear I cannot admire the names you propose to give the Baby," she wrote to the Prince of Wales after the birth of his second son in 1865. "I had hoped for some fine old name. Frederick is however the best of the two ... George only came in with the Hanoverian family." The Prince stuck to his guns and opted for George, who himself, when he was grown up, found a letter on his dressing table at Windsor in which Queen Victoria informed him that it was her dearest wish that he should call himself Albert. But he refused to change his own names round. "I had been christened George, and George I would remain," he explained.

He was then Duke of York, and though generally biddable was clearly unafraid of his matriarchal grandmother. When his eldest son

was born she insisted again on Albert for the first name on the grounds that "this will be the Coburg line" – the line founded in Great Britain by the Prince Consort. The Duke of York refused again: he and his wife had determined to call the baby Edward, after the Duke's elder brother who had died of pneumonia a couple of years earlier. When, however, the Yorks' second son was born, the misfortune of his having arrived on the very anniversary of the Prince Consort's death gave the Queen what she had wanted. To assuage her grief (the date was also the anniversary of her second daughter's death) the Duke of York, prompted by his father, offered to call the newly-born Albert. Victoria's approval was surprisingly qualified: "It is a great pleasure to me that he is to be called Albert, but in fact he could hardly be called by any other name," she wrote. The Duke's mother-in-law weighed in with a more prophetic comment. She disliked the name Albert and reflected that "George will be his last name, and we hope it may some day supplant the less favoured one." It did: the baby became King George VI.

The Duchess of York, though at the receiving end of these tiresome exchanges, was no less involved when some of her own grandchildren were born. As Queen Mary, she was not slow to dispense her advice and opinions. "Robert of Gloucester sounds well," she suggested to the Duke of Gloucester in 1942, following the birth of the baby who was nevertheless christened William. She tried again in 1944: "I hope this time," she wrote, "you will call him Richard, which sounds so well with Gloucester." The Duke reluctantly conceded. Fourteen years earlier Queen Mary had consulted her husband over the question of a name for their second granddaughter. The baby's mother – the present Queen Mother – had tactfully written to Queen Mary to sound out the reception for Ann Margaret, since Ann of York sounded "pretty" and several people had suggested Margaret. The reply came back that King George V was not in favour, and the names finally chosen were Margaret Rose.

So tradition and precedent indicate that the choice of royal names is not solely a matter for parents. But it is unlikely that the

present Queen proffered more than a tentative suggestion or two in the case of Prince William – and in a much more tactful way than Queen Victoria. Prince Charles in any event has a sufficiently deep sense of family and dynastic history to have acted as guardian of its traditions, while his wife may have helped to arrange the chosen

Surprise, surprise. Diana turns up for Royal Ascot on 16th June (bottom) and goes on to watch Charles playing polo again at Windsor.

names to avoid their sounding altogether too old-fashioned. For the future, the effort of selecting suitable names should not be so great: subsequent children born to the royal couple will, as their position in the line of succession allows, be given names free from the automatic influence of history and more in line with personal preferences.

The choice of godparents for Prince William offered another opportunity to modify old traditions. The usual practice of honouring

members of the family at such times has had its drawbacks in the past: of Prince Charles' six godparents three were so old that they were unlikely to be of any real value as mentors in the formative years, and their similar backgrounds offered little prospect of comprehensive guidance. Prince Charles, whose influence in the choice of his son's godparents is transparently evident, has gone

A leisurely chat between Charles and Diana after the game. Charles, as always, clutches a jar of sugar lumps—his usual reward for his horses.

some way to avoid such pitfalls. The accent, if not on youth, is unarguably on as young a generation as possible consistent with the benefits of experience, and while the range is by no means totally cosmopolitan, there are some interesting elements which may yet redound to the young Prince's character and orientation in the important years ahead.

The immediate Royal Family is represented solely by Princess Alexandra, the 45-year-old cousin of the Queen, likeable, informal and married to a businessman of considerable experience. Prince Philip's family is represented by ex-King Constantine of Greece, the Hampstead-based exile of some 15 years from the country he ruled for only three. He is Prince Charles' second cousin, and a close friend

with more immediate connections with the Danish royal house, his wife being the sister of Queen Margrethe. Another second cousin of Prince Charles – Lord Romsey – became godfather as representative of the Mountbatten family: he was also a contemporary of the Prince at Gordonstoun, and is the present owner of Broadlands, where the royal couple spent the first three days of their honeymoon. The last of the three male godparents is Laurens van der Post, whom Prince Charles met and admired in the course of his anthropological studies. A former soldier, and now a writer and journalist, he was

born in South Africa and is believed to have inculcated his notably anti-racialist views into Prince Charles, to whom he has long been a friend and mentor. The two remaining godmothers are the Duchess of Westminster, wife of Britain's richest aristocrat, whose daughter has Prince Charles for a godfather, and Lady Susan Hussey – a surprising but enlightened choice, for it was she who, as the Queen's senior lady-in-waiting, coached the then Lady Diana Spencer in the traditions and protocol of established royalty, and who was thus

Togetherness. Diana, who the previous week gave the lie to the belief that she disliked polo, makes her last public exit before her baby's birth five days later. The novel experience of the first pregnancy was about to end— and obviously on a note of great personal happiness.

responsible for her successful emergence as the wife of a Prince of Wales so universally liked, that at one stage it was difficult to imagine that any wife would be good enough for him.

For most people, godparents are at worst an irrelevancy; at best a quaint, ritualistic luxury with little after-value except as the source of birthday and Christmas gifts until coming-of-age takes over. But in some quarters the obligations are expected and assumed with considerable seriousness, and in the upper reaches of society the

practice of sponsorship for baptism brings with it the means of providing useful or influential social connections. Now it may be argued that members of the Royal Family are the last people to need social connections to be made for them, but is it really so? Fifty years ago, it is true, people looked to their Royal Family with reverence, wonder and envy, considering its born members ineffably privileged and those who married into it unspeakably fortunate. Today, a process of levelling – intellectual rather than material – leaves the roles in an uneasy balance. Few ordinary citizens would confess to "wanting their job for the world." The sight, for instance, of Lady Diana being all but thrown to the photographers appalled as much as it provoked curiosity, and Prince William himself will be fair game for his eager public as soon as his pram first appears where that public has a right to be. The restrictions on what any member of his family can say or do, and their inability to dodge what they *must* say and do, cannot but seem to them unfair, for all that there are compensations. And as the new baby's life unfolds under the public's

unrelenting gaze, he too will have to watch his step, choose his words, give every incipient friendship a second thought – all with such regularity that the temptation will be (as it once was with his father) to shelter within the confines of his own familiar but claustrophobic surroundings. The consequent risk of moving out of touch with life outside must be substantially lessened by contact with a select group of godparents whose duty it is to help mould his life both within and without the royal circle. His public movements may remain restricted, his public speeches bland and tame, but intellectually it would be fatal in a fast-moving age for his opinions to be blinkered by the restraints and coloured by the prejudices of his position. Any number of godparents of different backgrounds and intellectual complexion must therefore offer prospective benefits, and in this case the net has been cast sufficiently wide for Prince William to harvest a useful and liberal outlook on life in the course of

Command appearance. Once Prince William's birth was announced, everyone demanded to see the proud father. Charles eventually appeared an hour later, pleased as Punch and keen to share his delight with the crowd. They were thrilled with the reward of their long vigil.

his upbringing.

The unmerciful glare of publicity customarily trained on all princes, is one aspect of Prince William's upbringing which will be assimilated with the utmost difficulty. Getting used to it all will call for a measure of understanding which in other children would be labelled precocious. Realising why it all happens and what it signifies will involve considerations at least as confusing as those which Prince Charles fought manfully to master. "It's something that dawns on you with the most ghastly, inexorable sense . . ." he once said, and

Distinguished guests. The Queen and Earl Spencer signal their joy as grandparents again. Toastmaster Ivor Spencer and Paddington Bear muscle in. "There's a lot of happiness up there," said Diana's mother, and the appearance of the new parents with their son proved it.

he of all people will be concerned to see that the ultimate and inescapable dawning of the truth on his son is as painless as possible.

If this is to be the case, it is difficult to envisage how such aims can be squared with the oft-mooted rumour that the Princess of Wales intends – and has insisted – that her baby should accompany his parents if and when they go on foreign tours. The hare was raised in March with a newspaper story that she had presented the Queen with an ultimatum, refusing to undertake any foreign journeys unless accompanied by her child. The report was supposedly reinforced by an anonymous friend's confirmation that "Diana is not prepared to suffer emotionally because of outdated royal traditions." A Palace spokesman dismissed the story as "pure speculation" adding that it was highly unlikely that the Princess would deviate from royal protocol.

Certain factors seemed to support the official denial. One was that, as no royal tour for 1983 had yet been decided upon (most lengthy tours take some two years to arrange) the Princess would have at least eighteen months to enjoy motherhood before being called away by the demands of duty. Another was that any ultimatum like the one alleged would have left her with the impossible dilemma of being away from Prince Charles if she insisted on staying at home, and away from her baby if she capitulated. However credible the rumour, the hard fact is that royal parents are frequently absent for long periods at uncomfortably early stages in their children's lives. Even in the recent past we have the example of the Queen's parents leaving her at eight months old to visit Australia, while Prince Charles was only six months old when Prince Philip left home to resume his Naval career, and only twelve months old when his mother also left to join him. The period between 1949 and 1952 was one of constant parental absence on naval or royal duties abroad, which must have been bewildering for a child of such tender years. We may also reflect on the number of birthdays which Prince Andrew has celebrated with his parents: as February has always been a month high on the list for State Visits abroad, the Prince can probably count the number on the fingers of one hand. These experiences make it understandable for the Princess of Wales to have misgivings about the balance between her maternal wishes and her obligations as a fully-occupied member of the Royal Family, and it is not the easiest equation to solve, particularly if her baby is to be protected from over-enthusiastic publicity.

A more sinister aspect of the young Prince's upbringing, quite apart from being surrounded by spectators gawping into the royal goldfish bowl, is that he will be accompanied every day of his life by his own personal detectives. The shadow of the gunman has not

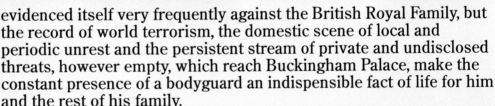

evidenced itself very frequently against the British Royal Family, but the record of world terrorism, the domestic scene of local and periodic unrest and the persistent stream of private and undisclosed threats, however empty, which reach Buckingham Palace, make the constant presence of a bodyguard an indispensible fact of life for him and the rest of his family.

In the child's earlier years, that ever-present detective will even oversee his daily outings with his nanny in Kensington Gardens – for it will be here that most of his excursions from home will take him. Only three weeks before he was born, his parents moved into Nos. 8 and 9 Kensington Palace – formerly two flats, but now converted into one – which will be their London home and office for the foreseeable future. Although the apartments have the benefit of a capacious private courtyard, there is no private garden, and Prince William's perambulator will therefore be seen in the adjoining parkland, the famous public haunt of all Knightsbridge nannies. At Kensington Palace the Prince will have no shortage of cousins for playmates. The two closest to his age-range will be Laura, the toddler daughter of the Princess of Wales' sister Lady Jane Fellowes – who lives at the Old Barracks at the southern end of the Palace grounds – and Lady Gabriela Windsor, the year-old daughter of Prince and Princess Michael of Kent, who also have apartments in the Palace. Their son, three-year-old Lord Frederick, may prove a little too old for Prince William, but Lady Rose Windsor, the two-year-old daughter of the Duke of Gloucester, will prove an energetic and forward companion and neighbour. When he is not at Kensington, Prince William will be at Highgrove, his parents' Gloucestershire retreat, but even here he will not be many miles away from his immediate Phillips cousins – four-year-old Peter and one-year-old Zara, the children of Princess

Anne.

One virtual certainty is that he will see much less of Buckingham Palace in his early years than his father did. Prince Charles was born there, lived within a quarter of a mile of it at Clarence House during his first three years, and frequently stayed there with his grandparents while his mother and father were away on State Visits on the King's behalf. After the Queen's accession in 1952, Prince Charles of course knew no other home. But Prince William's childhood and adolescence look set to be spent away from the formality and overwhelming grandeur of these immense headquarters of the British monarchy, though should Prince Charles be called to the Throne unexpectedly early, the young Prince's surroundings will suffer an unsettling change in consequence.

But the Queen is in excellent health and shows no sign of yielding to the lure of voluntary abdication. The odds favour a comparatively quiet upbringing for the Prince, who is unlikely to be spoilt by mollycoddling, since his mother, though patently maternal and at her doting best with children, seems to be a soft touch for no-one. Of his two parents his father looks like being the more indulgent, though whether he will find the time to cosset his children unduly is rather more questionable. At best, he might make time to write another book on the lines of "The Old Man of Lochnagar," sales of which have revived in the wake of his son's birth. For all that, there are signs that Prince Charles intends to be more than a mere part-time father, and that he will participate much more

The gentle touch of a mother, as Diana takes her baby from her solicitous husband. Less than twenty-four hours after his birth, Prince William first met his future subjects.

closely in his son's upbringing than may have been the custom in the past. During his wife's pregnancy he was busy reading up on the subject to the point where she remarked, almost ruefully, that he was "beginning to think himself something of an expert." He was one of the very few royal fathers ever – and the first since Prince Albert – to be purposely present at his son's birth, and would probably do it again even though, as he admitted afterwards, "it was a bit of a shock to my system." Nor has he made any secret of his pride and satisfaction on achieving fatherhood: his delightfully proud appearance from the privacy of the hospital, holding his son and heir in his arms said it all. He would be hard put to give more convincing

He was the first direct heir to the Throne to have been born in hospital and the Lindo Wing became a household name. Nevertheless the Princess couldn't wait to get home again.

notice that he will follow the modern trend and not leave all the day-to-day details of his son's future in the hands of others, however competent.

The pattern of that future is impossible, in these days of fluid and rapid change, to predict: certainly no-one has yet ventured a forecast to compare in scope, if not in content, with the uncannily accurate Kier Hardie when, in 1894, he outlined the downfall of Edward VIII. The boldest prognostications, outside the realms of astrology, have hardly gone further than random, and not very conclusive, thoughts on the size of the baby's ears, the shape of his nose, the speed with which he will grow hair, and lose it again, and how dazzling his smile will be. There is every temptation to stop at this comparatively trivial stage, and consider it an achievement to have got so far. The changes which Prince Charles' generation has witnessed are already considered to be phenomenal, but the lesson of history teaches us that they are nothing to those which will take place by the end of the century – when, incidentally, Prince William comes of age. Any attempt to foresee even the general circumstances in which his character will blossom, and the setting for his future public life, is almost immediately doomed to failure at a time when the Treasury and the Bank of England cannot even agree on something as comparatively close as next year's rate of industrial output.

We have, above all, no notion of how our social attitudes may have altered in the course of the next generation, or of what sort of

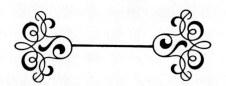

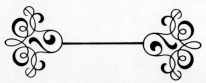

and new approaches, maintained by the replacement of faulty parts and the disposal of those which have outlived their usefulness, and polished by the popularity which surrounds its still decorative exterior. That general care and maintenance has been carried out with varying degrees of publicity during the present reign, and the next generation of operatives are sufficiently enlightened and intelligent to ensure that the process continues in step with contemporary demands. If fate permits, Prince William Arthur Philip

Held on 26th July, after many of the troops had returned on HMS Hermes, the service was attented by the Queen, Prince Philip, the Queen Mother and thirteen other members of the Royal Family.

Louis, 1982's prestigious royal arrival, will, as King William V, take over from them. As he lies in the cast-iron cradle of history, unknowing and unsuspecting of his destiny, those who wish the monarchy well must also wish that he enjoys a happy, successful, and above all a useful life.

First published in Great Britain 1982 by Colour Library International Ltd.
©1982 Illustrations and text: Colour Library International Ltd.,
    Guildford, Surrey, England.
Colour Separations by FER-CROM, Barcelona, Spain
Display and text filmsetting by ACESETTERS LTD., Richmond, Surrey, England.
Printed and bound in Barcelona, Spain by RIEUSSET and EUROBINDER
All rights reserved.
ISBN 0 86283 032 X

COLOUR LIBRARY INTERNATIONAL

D.L.B.: 22803